GOLDEN
MESSAGES
from the
ANIMALS

SILVIA NEFF

BALBOA.
PRESS

A DIVISION OF HAY HOUSE

Balboa Press books may be ordered through booksellers or by contacting:

Balboa Press
A Division of Hay House
1663 Liberty Drive
Bloomington, IN 47403
www.balboapress.com
1 (877) 407-4847

Because of the dynamic nature of the Internet, any web addresses or links contained in this book may have changed since publication and may no longer be valid. The views expressed in this work are solely those of the author and do not necessarily reflect the views of the publisher, and the publisher hereby disclaims any responsibility for them.

The author of this book does not dispense medical advice or prescribe the use of any technique as a form of treatment for physical, emotional, or medical problems without the advice of a physician, either directly or indirectly. The intent of the author is only to offer information of a general nature to help you in your quest for emotional and spiritual well-being. In the event you use any of the information in this book for yourself, which is your constitutional right, the author and the publisher assume no responsibility for your actions.

Any people depicted in stock imagery provided by Thinkstock are models, and such images are being used for illustrative purposes only.
Certain stock imagery © Thinkstock.

Print information available on the last page.

ISBN: 978-1-5043-8069-0 (sc)
ISBN: 978-1-5043-8070-6 (hc)
ISBN: 978-1-5043-8097-3 (e)

Library of Congress Control Number: 2017907735

Balboa Press rev. date: 05/19/2017

CONTENTS

This book is written with words of love. It is about my own experiences, which I would like to pass on.

I dedicate it to the animals, especially my two loved and loving dogs, Benny and Chico, who went over the Rainbow Bridge. They helped me to clearly recognize my healing journey and visibility, as well as to follow my path and my vocation. Through them, I realized how strikingly beautiful it is to connect with heart energy and to communicate through it.

I am also dedicating this book to the people who are entrusting their messages to me, which I hope to convey.

INTRODUCTION

Autumn 2016

I am sitting in my favorite spot in nature, a place called Loisachblick. From this place, I have a view above my nice small village. I am enjoying a last warm day before tomorrow's cold weather forecast. Tears roll over my face, and grasshoppers try to cheer me up. A dragonfly lands in front of me on a blade of grass and shimmers a beautiful golden green. She wants to comfort me with her grace. The memories of my little dog Chico touch me deeply.

How often did I walk with him? Three hundred times or more? I think more. Now all is empty; nothingness surrounds me. I feel him—I feel he is here—and yet there is no trace of his body. I miss caressing him; I miss the many beautiful experiences we had while walking together. In my thoughtful silence, I hear him barking, and I see him standing in front of me. Chico went back to the light on February 21, 2016, but I am still not recovered.

I am a passionate animal communicator. It is my calling, and it fills me with joy. I talk to animals, including those who are already on the other side in the light. I am in daily conversation with Chico. We are connected by our heart energy. He told me that he was doing well and that there was nothing missing. He has found a lot of friends. But can one forget the physical loss of a beloved four-legged comrade? No. The pain pierces your heart. I accept this process.

On the side of the rest area, I see a kind of mailbox with a book you can leave behind. I draw it to myself and dedicate a few lines to Chico.

On my way home, I listen to the birds. I spot a white feather in front of me. I get up and take it with me. A sudden stormy wind blows the last autumn leaves from the tree.

I listen and listen to Chico as he speaks to me: *My love, you will soon understand that everything has a meaning. I'm very close to you. When you are in doubt, you can ask me, and I will give you tremendous energy. You will follow your calling. With words you will break the chains, abide in your strength, and go your way.*

Chico sent me the picture of a book, and then I realized I am writing that book. It will allow me to bring the important messages of animals to the whole world.

CHAPTER 1

MY CHILDHOOD: A NURSE ON FOUR PAWS

My earliest contact with animals was with a nurse on four paws.

When Mommy would drive me in the stroller, a friendly German shepherd dog named Axel walked to my right, guarding me. Mom would leave me in the stroller in front of the bakery and disappear into it, knowing that I was safely under Axel's protection. He looked watchfully at everything. I thought he was great, and I showed him my toy teddy. He licked me with his tongue, making me laugh. Mom would come back and praise our great four-legged nurse who watched me so well.

Axel, our dear dog, really seemed to understand me. We would roll together on the ground and have our fun. I enjoyed growing up with all sorts of animals: there were budgerigars, dogs, hamsters, and cats. Our cats were well educated by my father. When they approached the birds, a whistle from Father was enough; the cats were on the spot and stopped the chase. I watched with a smile. Most of the time, the cats came to my lap to get a little love.

Our animals had beautiful lives. They were integrated and respected as family members. Our budgerigar, Putzi, was free to fly about. One Sunday at lunch, he landed on Dad's mashed potatoes. He did not want to miss such a pleasurable meal.

Cats and dogs slept in the children's room and, of course, in our bed. We children were not afraid of burglars, nor did we have bad dreams. We did not need a teddy bear to fall asleep. We had our pets. Our granddaddy's great Saint Bernard dog was happy to play with us, and we were allowed to sit on his back once. The dog was proud of this.

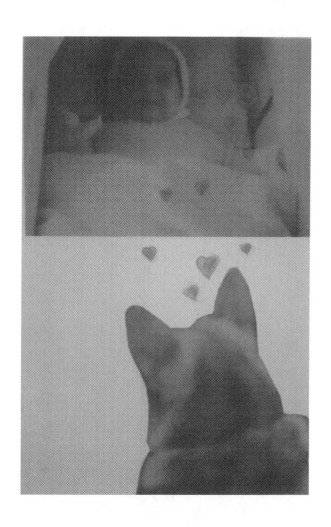

CHAPTER 2

EXCURSION TO THE ZOO

When I was four years old, our parents took us to the zoo. My big brown eyes could not get enough of it. There were so many animals!

The monkeys meant very much to me, and I would have liked to spend more hours there. I found them uncannily childlike and playful. My parents wanted to go on, so I said goodbye with the words, "Rejoice, you funny monkeys! Have so much fun."

On the opposite side were the llamas. When my parents got a little careless and lost sight of me for a minute, I took advantage of this opportunity and ran across to the llamas. I watched them as they moved. A llama came very close to me at the railing. She munched her grass while I said, "How are you? I am on a trip today." She turned her head sideways as if she was listening to me.

About fifteen minutes later, my parents found me. I took my leave of the llama, and I felt as if she had been talking to me for a long time. I didn't know that llamas spit, and the llama at the zoo did not spit. Why should an animal spit at me? I was her friend.

CHAPTER 3
A COW NAMED KERSTIN

Our parents could not afford a luxury holiday, but they were eager to spend some time with us and have fun in a beautiful environment. One time, Father rented a small bungalow on a farm for us. The farm was a bit off the road, surrounded by a green meadow. There were a large number of happy, grass-eating cows. Early in the morning, we were awakened by the bells and the low moos of these cows.

For breakfast, there were organic products directly from the farm that were especially fresh. Even the bread was baked there. The farmer offered us a large selection, including eggs from a happily free-range flock of chickens; homemade fruit spreads; honey from the neighbor's apiary; and butter, milk, yogurt, and cheese from the farm itself. We all had large portions of the delicious breakfast.

Right on the first day after that fantastic breakfast, I wanted to go on my own discovery trip. I waited for the right moment to escape from my parents. In the immediate vicinity was the cow pasture, and it called to me. Immediately, I crept under the fence and found myself amidst the many cows that pleasantly and serenely fed on the fresh green grass.

Beside me was an impressive cow with beautiful, curving horns. She gently chewed the fresh grass from the pasture. Neither her horns nor her greatness drove me to fear. After I stroked her, she licked my hand with her rough, long tongue, and then we were both immediately sympathetic. I found her fascinatingly beautiful and called her Kerstin.

While I stroked Kerstin, I started talking to her, and it seemed to me that she understood every word of mine, and I hers. You could say it was a friendship at first sight. Unfortunately, I had to separate from her, because my parents found me too early. I waved to her and was already looking forward to my next visit.

CHAPTER 4
THEN CAME BENNY

I grew up in the familiar surroundings of animals and developed from a girl to a sporty, life-embracing, and enterprising woman. After completing high school, I worked for a very qualified doctor. He used a lot of natural methods of healing, and I was trained and got my diploma as a medical specialist. A few years later, in an effort to expand my expertise, I took a position in surgery in the hospital of our city.

At the age of twenty-eight, I began a new step in my life. I got married, and as my husband and I had a house and a big garden, I decided to have a dog. I had enough time to spend with the dog with my reduced working hours and half-day job at the hospital.

Shortly afterward, in April 1997, I discovered in the newspaper an advertisement from a farm that would be giving up young golden retriever puppies. After a telephone discussion with the owner of the farm, I made my way there. Full of joy, I was greeted by a bustling bunch of young puppies. Even before I started to think of which of these cute puppies I would choose, a small puppy joined me and bit into my shoelaces with joy. It was clear that he was the right one for me. This little puppy wanted me.

Since the puppies were not old enough to leave the farm, my little prince named Benny was reserved for me. I was allowed to take him home two weeks later.

CHAPTER 5

BENNY, MY TEACHER

Benny grew up to be a lovely, beautiful golden retriever. We enjoyed our time together. He loved riding with me in the car. As soon as I came home from work, he would give me an overwhelming greeting. It didn't take long before he was standing in front of the trunk of my car, waiting to jump in.

For him, traveling in a car was fascinatingly beautiful. I called the car a driving dog hut. So we both had our fun. Very often we discovered beautiful places in nature. I always paused for us to relax during our walks. We were a well-trained team.

More and more, we grew together. He showed me the suns of life, fun, joy, playing, and nature, and I was no longer alone. Over time, he pointed me to a new path in life. It was time to let go of the old and open new doors. So it happened that after seven years of marriage, I decided to divorce, and I separated from my husband. We had different goals, and we separated in friendship. Benny, of course, went with me.

My apartment search was not easy. The many phone calls and inquiries were unsuccessful. No landlord accepted dogs. I learned by heart the answers that I began to expect: *Dog—no! No pet! We do not want a dog. What—a dog? No dogs scratching the ground.*

One morning, I went to a real estate office. After reading the advertisements, I saw an apartment I liked especially well, and I wanted to see it. But before I decided on this apartment, I saw in the small print a note: "No pets." With a deep sigh, I left the office building and undertook a long walk with Benny. I told Benny about the apartment but that I would rather stay in a tent than be without him.

Benny looked at me calmly, and then he telepathically told me that this apartment I had found at the real estate agent was destined for us both. I thought for a little bit, but I knew Benny was right. I arranged for a visit to this apartment.

When the real estate agent showed me the apartment, I was speechless. It was beautiful, with a small balcony, a little garden, a bedroom, a living room, a small kitchen, and a large bathroom. It appeared optimal for Benny and me. The real estate agent was managing the apartment for an entrepreneur who had lived far away for a very long time. He did not care about who was in the apartment; for him, it was only important that the person was friendly and the rent was paid regularly.

My intuition and Benny's testimony gave me a good feeling. It was clear to me that this entrepreneur, my landlord, had nothing against pets, and I signed the contract. I wanted to report to the landlord and inform him of my dog without the real estate agent knowing. After signing the contract, I was given the key. The real estate agent knew nothing about my dog.

The very next day, I brought the first moving boxes into my new apartment. Benny was there. He trotted beside me. It was not long before we were greeted by the caretaker and organizer of the building. He saw Benny and laughed, with the words, "Is he yours?"

I said yes.

The caretaker replied, "That's nice."

Dogs were welcome in this residential complex. Here there were many dogs. I was very happy and hugged my Benny. He was right again. Shortly thereafter, I phoned my new landlord and had a very pleasant conversation on the phone. He was glad to have me as a tenant, and my dog, Benny, was welcome.

CHAPTER 6

A TRIP TO ITALY

Benny was a real comedian and actor. I remember one time I was to accompany my friend Gisela to Lake Garda. Everything was organized for our trip. My acquaintances wanted to take care of the dog, but Benny wanted to come along, and that was my wish.

The hotel did not allow dogs, and my girlfriend had already booked our reservation. Gisela was very often in this hotel, and she wanted to invite me. The cancellation fee was 80 percent.

So I talked with Benny and told him I would like to have him with, but I had no idea what the solution might be. With a smile, he told me that I did not have to worry about anything. He was coming with us.

The day before our trip, Benny limped. He could hardly walk, and my acquaintances did not want to take over this responsibility. They liked Benny, but not in Benny's bad condition. They were too scared. I could not see a wound, and I was sure Benny was only slightly sprained. Still, I accepted the doubts and fears of my acquaintances.

My curative and holistic practitioner for pets gave me good homeopathic remedies for him. Then I described the incident to my friend, Gisela. She took all the steps necessary to take Benny with us. We convinced the hotel that he was an exceptionally good, quiet dog, and they accepted him. The ride started, and we lifted the hobbling dog into the car.

As we crossed the border to Italy, we paused at a petrol station. Benny jumped out of the car with cheerful and joyful well-being—and no trace of hobbling.

He grinned at me. With a smile, I told him he was a great actor, and I was glad he was there.

CHAPTER 7
BENNY AND MY TRIP TO HAWAII

Benny's unquestionable serenity fascinated me more and more every day. He moved me to it. As time passed, I became more concerned with my spiritual growth and my creative way of life. I pursued this through books, workshops, and social media. I meditated a lot, spent a lot of time in nature, and heard more and more the calling of my inner voice, which told me I should go on a trip to Hawaii.

Hawaii was a fascination for me. A book about Lemuria, a sunken island in the Pacific—the present Hawaii— aroused a longing in me. I absolutely wanted to discover this spiritual and mystical Hawaii, and I was sure I was rooted in this land before many incarnations.

Although I understood Benny very well, I was not quite sure how he would manage staying with my parents for my long trip of four weeks. He assured me he would be fine. Benny had been there very often and was well taken care of. I worried, though, that while he would accept my long absence, he might suffer inwardly.

I contacted a dear friend who was a very good, experienced animal communicator. Perhaps Benny would have something to tell her that he did not dare tell me, so as not to hurt me. But my dear friend confirmed that Benny would agree with the parental accommodation.

This removed my last doubts and showed me that my communication with Benny was accurate. Now, through my time in Hawaii, the strength of that would build and intensify.

With Benny situated, I went on my trip to Hawaii. When I got off the plane in Maui, I knew it would be a good experience. Maui was a powerful paradise with many mystic places that impressed me very much.

Benny and my trip to Hawaii

Throughout my time in Hawaii, I was very often

telepathically connected to Benny. I remember well when I asked him once during my trip how he was, and he immediately gave me a picture of a white sausage called *Weisswurst*. This sausage is a traditional favorite, but it does not come so often on the menu. This day, my mother was cooking it for lunch, and Benny got a big piece of it.

It had also snowed a lot that day. Benny was playing in the garden, rolling in the snow and enjoying himself.

A little later, I phoned Mama. At that time, there were still public telephones distributed everywhere on the street. I said to her, "Well, today you had Weisswurst, and how are you managing with the snow?" She wondered how I knew that—did I call Papa before? I smiled and told her, "No, my dear Mama, that was Benny."

Hawaii

Maui gave me a lot of gifts. Most of the time I was at sea and in nature. I got a lot of knowledge about Maui and its culture from the local people. I discovered many mystical powers. I observed a whale, enjoyed the view on the Haleakala crater, and was impressed by the many simultaneous rainbows over the Pacific. Through these many gifts, I found myself in calm and balance, and I could communicate well with Benny and other animals.

Nevertheless, by the third week, I was longing for my family—and, of course, for Benny. I could hardly wait to cuddle him again

On the day of my return home, I told Benny telepathically that I was now on my way back to him and looking forward to seeing him. Benny was just as excited as I was. I could not sleep on the plane, despite my fatigue.

After a long journey, I landed in Munich. It was still a good hour by car to reach my parents' house. When I got there, Benny was already waiting at the door. What a welcome! He was overjoyed by my return, and we both lay on the ground for hours. I could hardly stop cuddling him.

My niece had joined us, and she told me that Benny had not slept or eaten all night. He kept on barking and running about restlessly. I told her, "He knew I was coming home."

Despite my jet lag, I went for a walk with Benny. There was a lot of snow, and he rolled in it. We had stayed very close despite the long journey and distance.

CHAPTER 8

BENNY WENT OVER THE RAINBOW BRIDGE INTO THE LIGHT

The heart connection between Benny and me grew constantly. Without words, we caught the emotions of the other. A look was enough, and he understood me.

As he grew older, every now and then he gave me a paw, and I realized he had pain in his body. Through his physical afflictions and our telepathic level, he explained to me that he was slowly starting his journey into the light.

The spiritual world and Benny showed me a sign of the announced going into the light on a gloomy summer afternoon. There was a huge rainbow above us. The next day, the redemptive transition to the light was carried out by the veterinarian as Benny slept on my lap.

It broke my heart. Even though Benny will always be connected with me on the spiritual plane, this transition was new. Benny gave me confidence, and I felt his presence.

He was not quite sure at the beginning whether he wanted to incarnate again. He needed a certain time to feel well in his new light body. But then he was given a new position by the spiritual world, and he decided to take this position with honor and joy. It was now shared with me in the role of guide and soul-companion. He would convey to me messages of love and growth from the light side. I could rely on him that he would always be at my side and help me with advice and action.

Thus, he is always present and immediately on the spot. Benny's messages are handed over to me in an empathic way, and they arrive truthfully. It is fascinating, and I will describe it in greater detail in this book.

CHAPTER 9

MY HEALING JOURNEY
TO PORTUGAL

The confidence, understanding, and communication with Benny in the light reduced a bit of my grief and pain. Nevertheless, I missed him. Benny told me that it was time for me to recover and sent me a picture of the sun, the Atlantic, and the words, "a journey to Portugal."

The next day, I followed Benny's recommendation. I was lucky and booked—after the spontaneous leave application was signed by my boss—a cheap flight package that included a hotel in Portugal, where it was warm early November.

When I was waiting for the plane at Munich Airport, I held back tears. I was emotionally moved by the longing for Benny. I couldn't imagine, in my present dismal situation, that Portugal would be able to relieve this pain. But Benny whispered to me, "This journey will be your cure."

After a quiet flight, I landed in Faro, and then I went by bus to my hotel in Albufeira. It was, as described, the so-called Martinssommer, and still pleasantly warm. I enjoyed the bus ride and the impressive, beautiful scenery. After checking in at my hotel, I went to the beach, which was right outside the hotel. I listened to the Atlantic and wondered what Benny wanted to tell me.

I heard the soothing sound of waves, and then I heard his voice: "Portugal will turn your life on its head."

I had a very nice room with a sea view and a large balcony. There I came to rest and listen to the roar of the waves, the barking of the neighbor dogs, and the shrieking of seagulls. I thanked Benny for these impressive first pictures of my trip and fell asleep.

After a good night's sleep, I was awakened by a sunbeam shining through the room. I could hardly stop for breakfast; I was so moved to get outdoors. The sun was shining in a cloudless sky, and the temperature was about 22 degrees Celsius. I grabbed my bathing bag and went down to the beach.

CHAPTER 10

A FOUR-LEGGED SURPRISE

Shortly after I left the hotel, I crossed a small parking lot. Suddenly, I stood rigid as a statue. My heart pounded extremely quickly. There lay a little street dog hidden in a hollow between two parked cars. He looked at me, shy and frightened. I leaned down gently to him and stroked him carefully.

"Who are you, my little one?" I asked gently. "Do not you have a mom or a dad?" It seemed to me as if he had been waiting for me, and it was pleasant to him when I touched his coat carefully with my hand. Tourists passed, ignoring me and the dog.

I wanted to buy the small dog food, but I did not know if he would stay there until I found a supermarket and came back again. I said to him, "Little boy, please wait for me. I'll buy food quickly, and I will be back with you."

The next small supermarket was about five minutes away, and I ran as fast as I could. Fortunately, there was a last can of dog food. Even though I waited longer at the checkout than planned, the little dog had understood me and waited patiently.

When he saw me opening the can, he yelped with joy and jumped up to me. He was very hungry and quite emaciated. A small black cat joined us, and the cat also got some food.

After I fed the little dog, he thanked me with a loving, touching look. My heart was melting. I brought him with me into the green area by the bungalows of the hotel. We lay there for an hour, and it seemed to me that I had my own little son with me in my lap—a feeling I had missed so long.

We were so close to each other, although we had only known each other for a short time. A maid of the hotel watched us. As she went on her way to clean the bungalows, she said to me, "Finally, a dear lady who cares about him. He's been on the road for a long time." She told me her husband would call the dog Francesco—Chico for short. it was clear to me that I would call the little street dog Chico too. It suited him. It was a short name, and he would understand that when I called him.

Chico slept next to me there on the green. He was pretty tired and finally fully fed. I let him sleep. The maid promised that she would take care of little Chico for me so I could enjoy the beach a bit. I gave the maid some money and went briefly to the beach. When I came back, little Chico was still there. He was waiting for me, and he followed me to the hotel.

Unfortunately, I was not allowed to take him into the hotel. I telepathically told him that I would visit him again soon and bring food. He looked at me, and I was sure that he understood me.

CHAPTER 11
HELP FROM THE LIGHT SIDE

I made my way to dinner and was seated with a lady who was traveling alone. I had a pleasant conversation with her. Because of my food plan and selection of dishes, it was clear to her that I was a vegetarian. After I took my dessert, we said goodbye. I wrapped a big piece of chicken fillet and cooked beef fillet in my napkin when I left the dining room, and the lady looked at me with a bit of surprise—especially when I left the hotel with the servants.

It was already dark outside. I looked for Chico, but he was not there. He had probably crawled away. Because of the many passing cars, this was a dangerous place for him. Based on an injury and scar on his hind limb, he'd already had a bad experience with the road traffic.

With loud shouts of his name, I went toward the bungalow facilities. I also tried to contact him telepathically. Suddenly, there was a rustling in the bushes behind me, and there was Chico. He greeted me with great joy, and he devoured the meat I had brought to him with delight.

I took him into my room that night, although I knew it was not allowed. I hid him in my bathing bag and crept past the front desk. I prepared Chico a little bed in my room. I had contacted through the Internet a lady who cares for stray street dogs in Portugal, and she said she would call me the next day to help me further. Chico fell asleep with me. I stroked him for a long time before my eyes fell.

At about four o'clock in the morning, I was awakened by the barks of other dogs who were out in the open. Chico started to whine. I immediately understood that they were also street dogs, and they were looking for Chico. I put on jogging pants and a shirt and went outside with him. I hid him so that he was not seen from the front desk.

Out in the open, he ran toward the bungalows and further into a green environment of nothing but bushes. He told me to follow him, and I did. Then he entrusted me with his secret hiding places. He told me he was going to see his friends now. I said goodbye to him and went to my hotel. *Good night, dearest, see you soon.* He looked at me for a moment and ran away.

The next day, I spoke on the phone with Rita, the lady I had found through the Internet. She went with me to a recording station for dogs nearby. It was run by a warm and loving Swedish lady and her husband. Of course, I wanted to take Chico there for his safety. I also realized that I wanted take him to Germany. I definitely knew we'd stay together, and I also knew that Benny had led me to Chico.

Before he could travel abroad, Chico needed medical care and injections. That was why I agreed with Rita to take him to the Swedish family's house to get him well. Rita took care of the taxi and said I should call her the next day when Chico came back to me.

The next morning, immediately after breakfast, I went

with my wrapped ham to the bungalow to feed Chico. Unfortunately, no Chico was to be seen. I called for him, and I went to his secret places, but no Chico. I saw how the garden had been remodeled by workers. They'd cut the hedge too.

I was afraid for Chico. What had happened to him? I had to look for him and find him. I only had four days until my flight back to Germany.

I paused, took a deep breath, and went back to my room. I tried to get in telepathic touch with Chico, but I could not. I was too excited and not in the relaxing, calm mood needed.

To find balance, I telephoned a dear friend from Germany. She calmed me with the words, "Silvia, there is an angel for the lost animals—Archangel Raphael. He is also the angel for travelers, the angel of healing, and the guardian angel of Portugal. In Portugal, there is a special light, and through this light you will be connected with Archangel Raphael."

Yes, she had it right. This light was noticeable to me. It was a special light and fascinatingly bright.

After taking a rest. I asked Archangel Raphael for support, as well as my dear Benny. Then I went to look for Chico. I felt a warm familiar feeling and a bond with Chico. Somehow, Chico told me telepathically that he needed this time to say goodbye. He would come when the time was right.

I spent the whole day outdoors. I went through woods

and meadows and through isolated farms. I asked the locals if they had seen a little street dog. I did not give up.

With confidence that I would find him in time, I went to the beach. After dinner, I fell into a light sleep. The next day after breakfast, I looked out in the open for Chico. Unfortunately, there was no trace of him. A maid greeted me kindly, and she showed me a small cat family in the immediate vicinity. A cat had given birth to many small babies. I was happy to see them, but I was still a bit restless, because I missed my little Chico.

I continued to rely on the help from above and my telepathic contact with Chico. A couple from England who lived in a bungalow watched me, and they asked me if I had lost something and if they could help me. I told them about my adventures with Chico. The couple were animal lovers, and they wanted to help me with the search.

Even before I could thank the couple for their support, there was once again a rustling in the bushes, and there he was—Chico! I was so happy. He confirmed my suspicion and the familiar feeling that it was important for him to spend the rest of the time with his friends before he left this place. How relieved I was. My eyes were also directed upward into the light, and I thanked Archangel Raphael and my dear Benny. Through their trust, I could let go of my fear and doubt.

I then contacted Rita, who had been waiting a long time for my call. She arranged for a driver to take me to the recording room with Chico. Shortly thereafter, the taxi arrived, and Chico rode confidently with me in the car, as if he knew in advance that for him, a new life was beginning.

Now we went to the dog court, which was about forty-five minutes away. There we were received by the dear Swedish couple, Eve and Piere. They already had thirty dogs to provide for. All the dogs had been brought in off the road.

Chico was now taken into custody. Eva and Piere had already seen a lot of misery, and it was an important task for them to help the poor dogs. The lovely Eva wanted to leave Chico for the first time a little alone in the room and then bring him to the other dogs in the pack. Eve took such good care of him for this short time.

There was still a lot to discuss, for Chico was to be flown to Germany by an airliner. I thanked Benny. He had helped me very much to forget my grief and move forward on a new path.

CHAPTER 12
CHICO COMES TO GERMANY

The next day, I enjoyed the beach and the sea, listened to the sound of the waves, and knew everything was good. Within a week, I was again shown how important it is to trust the inner voice and the spiritual world. One can certainly recognize connections even though they have not yet arrived.

One day before I went home, I visited Chico. When I rang the doorbell at the dog house, I was greeted by the lovely Eva along with Chico. He was very happy and jumped around, and that made me happy. Chico had already become well acquainted with the other dogs. Emma, a small dog lady, was particularly charming and took care of him.

I discussed with Eva the further procedure while Chico made himself comfortable on my lap. He was to be flown to Germany after the four-week vaccination interval with a young lady from Austria who had offered herself as a flight sponsor.

I spent the whole afternoon in the dog house. Eva told me about her many experiences, and how it had become their vocation to help street dogs. The dogs were well cared for and happy. In order to keep the whole thing under control, she tried to convey dogs to good places.

From that moment on, I became even more aware of how insignificant dog breeders are. You do not need them. You can find the best, greatest, and most grateful dogs without dealing with these businesses. They wait in the animal shelters and on the street. There are countless projects and organizations dedicated to helping helpless dogs find a good home.

When dawn approached, I took leave with tears in my eyes and Chico's and took a taxi back to my hotel. Chico looked after me. He knew we'd meet again. It is unbelievable how strong we had grown together in just one week.

As soon as I flew over Portugal, Benny joined me telepathically to assure me that my new life with a loving four-legged angel was well thought out and organized by the spiritual world. I thanked him for keeping his promise. How right Benny was again.

After a sunny week in bright Portugal, I landed in cool Germany. I had now almost four weeks to prepare everything for Chico. The next morning, I made my way to my neighbors. They used to be very concerned about Benny, and they had become for me the dearest neighbors in the world. They often gave me advice and helped me with tricky situations.

I told them about my experiences with Chico. I also asked for help. They were both in retirement and very animal-loving. I asked if they could take Chico for a few hours a day so that he was not long alone during my work time. They agreed to do it.

On December 5, 2008, Chico began his journey to his new home. I was so excited, and I drove two hours before arriving at the airport with heart palpitations. At home, everything was prepared. with a new basket, food, a small garden, and dear people who look forward to meeting him.

I looked at the clock and saw that the plane would soon land, After restlessly walking back and forth along the long corridor of the airport's arrival hall, I could finally see the landing of the plane from Faro on the arrival board. I took a deep breath. It was time.

The door opened, and a young lady with many boxes of dogs stood in front of me. Where was Chico? I looked at the many dog boxes, and … there he was! I ran to the young lady and immediately to the dog box where Chico was.

"Chico!" I called out. "I am so happy you are here!" He recognized me immediately and scratched the box. I let him out, and he jumped up at me. It did not look like he had a long day and a strenuous trip behind him.

This day, December 5, was for me an early Christmas.

My little Chico was back with me, and it was the most beautiful Christmas gift I'd ever had. I thanked the nice lady who was his flight sponsor for her great help with the flight, and then I went to the car with Chico. He ran well on the lead and followed me with the familiar feeling that he had finally found his home.

After an almost two-hour drive, we were home. It was after midnight, and we both walked a little round so Chico could get a first impression of his new home. Afterward, there was a delicious meal for him. Shortly after, he slept in his little basket, which was next to my bed. We both were very tired.

The next morning, we went to my neighbors after a long snoop round in the meadow behind my apartment. Chico ran perfectly on the lead. When my neighbors saw Chico they were moved. It would be a pleasure for them to take Chico into their care while I was working.

After a few weeks of getting him used to the cold season, I was able to run Chico without a line. He stayed with me and understood me very well. He felt very comfortable with the neighbors. Our communication and understanding became ever clearer and better. Also, Benny gave me to understand that he found Chico very great, and the two together in the same incarnation would be very good friends. Benny had brought us together, and the whole thing was going very well.

CHAPTER 13

TRANSFORMATION

With Chico, my life changed once again. Through his unconditional love, I learned the remaining fine art of animal communication.

The years passed and Chico grew older. At the beginning of 2016, he gave me clear hints he would like to go now. He was weak and wanted to break out. He had no more strength. On the other side, in the light, it would be very easy to accompany, guide, and support me.

I ignored this at first, since no serious illness was present. A veterinarian confirmed that. But then everything went very quickly. Within fourteen days, in the phase from the new moon to the full moon, we went together to the crossroads, because of a radical kind of blood cancer. He slept in my arms through salvation by the veterinarian. Chico gave me the exact time when I should call the veterinarian, and I accompanied him, so he went with all strength and love into the light.

On the other side, he was immediately received by my

beloved Benny. Chico with Benny in the light are from now on my guides and messengers. I receive messages from them daily.

I would like to present the most important messages of Benny and Chico in the light, and those of many dear animals. I would like to thank them again for allowing me to reveal these messages to the world in this book.

CHAPTER 14

LOVE INSTEAD OF FEAR

I would like to give this topic—love instead of fear—a special value in this book. Recently, the cosmos has given us many opportunities to love, to solve the old fears of the past and our childhood, and to let go of the patterns that our ancestors dragged along with them. It takes courage to look at these fears and not run away. To do this is a way of finally eradicating them.

It's all about recognizing yourself and loving yourself. Only when we respect and love ourselves can we be loved and accept love from others. The more love we allow, the less fear has a chance.

There are many ways to resolve these old fears— meditation, shamanic healing, sound massage, and prana breathing, to name a few examples. It just needs a conscious *yes, I can do it*. My path to anxiety relief was given to me by animal communication and the way of my vocation.

I have known this issue of anxiety very well. For years, I neglected my inner voice, listened to my ego, and allowed unfounded fears free rein. The result was weakness and failure.

Through my conversations with the animals, I was able to build stability. I switched off my thoughts, opened my heart chakra, communicated with the animals, followed the inner voice, and was connected with the cosmos and all of creation. After some time, it became routine. Now I trust it completely. It is a kind of broadcasting with creation.

After a hard day, it is a pleasure to be able to go in my retreat. I see it as my wellness program. My stress level falls, and I feel secure and powerful. During my animal talks, I am in harmonious company and perfect love with all. I treat myself with respect and regard all species and all creation with respect. Through my self-confidence, my life has changed, and I have a happy all-is-well feeling.

CHAPTER 15

A SPIDER TEACHES ME

Many people are disgusted by insects and especially by spiders. I too used to have that prejudice. It was broken through my conversations with these creatures. Very often I remember the touching conversation I had with a creeping spider.

My apartment is on the ground floor, and it has a terrace and a small garden that I visit often. Time outside helps me to relax and disconnect from stress. When opening the terrace door one nice late-summer day, I accidentally destroyed a spider's web. A spider had spun it right in front of the terrace door. I was sad that this masterpiece was broken.

The spider hung on one last thread, and I apologized to her with these words: "Dear spider, I am so sorry that I destroyed your net, but it was without intention."

She answered me wisely that she had watched me very often, and she knew I was on the bright side. Not only she but many other spiders felt comfortable with me. Before I cleaned the apartment with the vacuum cleaner, I would lovingly collect them and bring them outside into nature. I would never kill them; I treated them with respect.

Now this spider would weave a new net, as it was part of her life task and her home. I suggested that she should weave a little farther along the fence by the hedge, where nothing could happen. The next morning, a newly woven net was directly on the side of the fence I had proposed. Even though she was no longer in the windbreak and was shaken by the wind, she went uncompromisingly with my suggestion.

I thanked her for her prompt acceptance of my proposal. Since she was a very wise spider, I asked her if she could give me a message for the people as a recommendation. I said that I would be very grateful to her, and I would pass it on with pleasure. Immediately I received a message with the following words:

> You humans are just reaching a new dimension of consciousness. You will understand that we have preceded you in many situations. We are all connected in a network and together.

I knew she meant the Internet, and I understood her very well. Spiders deserve the same respect and honor as all of creation. Thank you, dear spider. I continue to observe this wise advice.

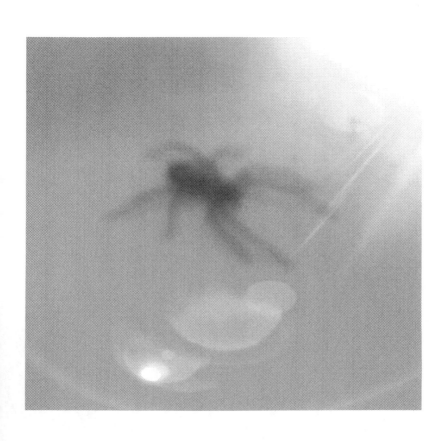

CHAPTER 16

EVERYTHING IS PERFECT
AND BARRY THE DOG

Barry—a lovable, blind dog—talked to me like a true philosopher. He was accustomed to his condition. His owner, Jessy, wanted to know if Barry could handle his blindness well. Barry told me that he stayed in balance by smelling, vibrating, and feeling. He took everything in very quickly and could do well. He wanted affection and caresses. He also told me the following:

> People have forgotten many things, and that is why I am here, as a small four-legged individual, to open your eyes despite my blindness. Live from the heart and feel! This works very well with eyes closed. We are all creation and perfect. The body only plays a small role. Feeling, especially love, does not need eyes. It is boundless. Allowing is important. Dear loved humans, let it flow

and it flows. You will enjoy this flow and
will feel good about it. You will perceive
the perfection, and then everything will be
perfect.

I was gripped by these dear words. Barry is, for me,
an angel in dog shape, and he deserves his strokes and
dedication in my book.

My experience has shown that animals have nothing
to complain about with their bodies—with the exception
of when people unnaturally change an animal. Animals
do not criticize themselves and do not judge any animal
by appearance or shape. They take it as it is and live in the
now. We can learn a lot from them.

CHAPTER 17

CINDY, A MOTHERLY, WARM-HEARTED HORSE

We humans have four bodies: the visible, tangible physical body; the emotional body; the mental body; and the spiritual body. When I connect with animals, I find myself outside of matter, in my spiritual body. It is possible to communicate with the animals on this level. Everything is energy.

The examples of Cindy and Fiffi clearly explain to me what energy means and how we deal with it. In this chapter, I will tell you about Cindy. When I first came into contact with her, she told me how much she had wanted to be the mother of a foal. Unfortunately, this was no longer physically possible. However, she had a loving owner who was a carer for children and very much in harmony with a holistic and spiritual way of life. She brought Mandy, a sweet young girl, as a riding participant. Through Mandy's childlike energy and a natural healing treatment, Cindy improved day by day.

Since Cindy is very sensitive, she was rather burdened by the energy of the barn. In the Middle Ages, there was a lot of suffering at this place. Cindy absorbed this energy and strained herself with it. She told me that she often felt weak. By turning her head, she tried to block the old energies in the barn. She loved to eat, and that would be a certain protection and an important measure.

Cindy was inspired by bright signs. Flower of life, positive energetic fodder, and complementary products made her feel well protected. Since then, her daily life has been stable, healthy, and fun.

CHAPTER 18

FIFFI AND THE ENERGY

When I happened to see Fiffi, a small terrier dog, during my jogging, he greeted me with joy. I was glad for his friendly welcome. His owners let me know that Fiffi very carefully selected his people. There were many people he liked who did not attach any importance to contact.

When I stroked him, I immediately realized that Fiffi was a very lively, cheerful creature with a mega antenna who could recognize and perceive energies. I named him Antenna Dog. I kept conversing with the owners, since they were very sympathetic, and I had in Fiffi an equal in the heart.

After my conversation with the owners, they asked me for an animal communication, because Fiffi would certainly have something to say. He was constantly barking, and this could be very tiring.

When I talked to the little one, he told me that he had grown up as a puppy in a surrounding area with people who gave him no love and affection. There was only darkness. He now was receiving the missing love and leading a good life with his new owners. He was a terrier, and he had a lot of energy. In addition, he absorbed any strange energy immediately and tried to block it by barking to protect his owners.

He was the little prince, and he had everything under control. He wanted to keep the house as safe as possible, and he did not like to be alone. Otherwise, he would lose control.

I told him about myself and that I was also an energy person, but sometimes serenity would be quite good, and he would certainly be fine with it. I recommended to the owners that they put healing stones in the house, such as rose quartz, to block foreign energies. That would make it easier for Fiffi to be relaxed.

Recently, I spoke with the owners on the phone. After our conversation, Fiffi had become quieter and had calmed down. How much I look forward to seeing Fiffi, the sweet Antenna Dog, again. He is so cute, and I hope to meet him again soon.

CHAPTER 19

HILDA THE TIGER

After my animal communication with the sweet cat Hilda, I realized how important it is to accept the shadow side of ourselves. We must accept it as a gift—and as a kick to resolve our no-longer-relevant fear-based patterns.

Hilda was a very bright, lovely, and sensitive cat. Her loving owners took care of her as well as possible. When her owners needed a break from work, they brought Hilda to a cat shelter so she would not be alone. She had a lot of spotting and a balcony in the cat board, but she could not go outside.

After fourteen days, she was picked up by her owners, and since then she had been constantly outdoors for mouse hunting. She gave me to understand that she had a lot of catching up to do. She was currently a tiger and had a strong desire to bring that to the surface.

I told her, "Wow, I had no idea! It seemed to me that you are more of a shy and sensitive kitten."

Hilda replied, "We all have a tiger in us. It is important

to accept this. We have light and shadow; we are active and passive. There is in nature the day and the night. Everything is in balance. We should also think about it. It makes no sense to suppress the tiger in us. He needs to have the right to come to the surface."

And how right she was. We will not develop into a beast, but we can also look at our pages of shadows. We all have these pages. If we consider and accept them, we can dissolve them. It is the way to light. It frees us, because we can only see through the shadow side to the light side. With this acceptance, we move forward into the light.

CHAPTER 20
THE ANIMAL AS YOUR REFLECTION

It is noticeable to me that the closer a pet comes into contact with the owner, the more disease symptoms (body or spirit) are transferred and take over. Although animals are authentic with the harmony of creation, they want to help a close person or owner with the dissolution of blockades.

The pet interferes with the functional disturbances of the animal owner—taking over, mirroring, or filtering the disturbance. By taking over the illness or blockade, the animal can draw the attention of the human being to his or her own illness or blockade. In my opinion, an animal loves unconditionally.

Katy, a lovable mare, became very tired and weak. She took in mold by eating dried grass. In addition, Katy was restless and nervous. She did not want to be on the paddock and could not concentrate.

At the same time, Britta, her owner, was treated because of a fungus in the intestine by a healing practitioner. In addition, Britta suffered from stress because of work and problems in a private area. Britta and Katy are very close. You could say the two are soul-related.

In this way, Katy took over the symptoms and emotions of her Britta. Through the good treatment of a healing practitioner, a better-organized job for Britta, and a renewed harmony in the partnership, Britta's physical and emotional state stabilized.

Shortly thereafter, a health check was carried out on Katy. In the results, healthy, germ-free, and mold-free intestinal mucus was found. Her medicine was discontinued. Katy was full of enthusiasm, showing no trace of nervousness or weakness. She had fun with life and riding.

CHAPTER 21

Take Everything Slightly Easier

After longing for years to return to the beautiful country of Portugal, I planned a holiday there with my partner. The country attracted me magnetically, especially because I had found my Chico there. The first day there, we watched the many seagulls who flew over us with loud noises, enjoying the beautiful, warm breeze by the sea. They felt well and happy.

At night, the gulls chirped and shouted and laughed cheerfully and sometimes woke us up from sleep. The so-called laughing gulls do not get their name for nothing. They made themselves known again the next day as we breakfasted on the terrace. Seagulls watched us most of the time.

Because of a soft mattress, I had overnight developed quite a back pain. So I sat at breakfast with a rather tense back. Then I heard from the rooftops the gulls copying me and playing me as comedy. The first gull seemed to say, "Au Au Au aua pain pain pain ..." The second gull followed up with "hahahaha." I immediately start laughing. The seagulls tried to ease my pain with their fun comedy, and they had mastered it successfully. Through my laughter, my back tension also loosened.

Seagulls are comedians and true jokers. The lightness, uncomplicatedness, and uninhibited playfulness of the gulls should teach us to take life slightly easier and become more relaxed. Even though we have grown out of childhood, we have an inner child. It longs for play, joy, and an uncomplicated way of life.

CHAPTER 22
MY ANIMALS AS MEDICAL SERVICE

I remember well when I went to the dentist with a pretty inflamed wisdom tooth. After the tooth-pulling, the dentist gave me an ice bag and a tamponade for my mouth and sent me home with the recommendation to rest in bed. This was not possible. A lively, joyful Benny was waiting at home for his outdoor walk. So I held the ice pack to my cheek, bit the tamponade in my mouth, and walked with him.

I could hardly concentrate on the pain, because I was infected by Benny's funny, uncomplicated naturalness. After our walk, neither swelling nor bleeding nor pain was present. I was doing well. When I went to the dentist for an examination the next day, he wondered at the enormous speed of wound healing.

Through emotions and cheerfulness, animals help people forget their pain, or at least ease their symptoms. Pets divert their owners from their physical as well as mental plagues. For myself, it has been a very effective method of healing.

Through Benny's uncomplicated behavior and absolute ignorance of my drawn wisdom tooth, I entered a serene energy that activated my body for self-healing. I was distracted, which meant I was not only physically but also emotionally in a state of consciousness far from suffering and illness. My cells took this state of consciousness and immediately set off to activate my self-healing powers.

For years I had physical problems with a mercury burden in my body. At that time, I had no idea about mercury's effects and about detoxification procedures at the dentist. I had amalgam tooth fillings removed without detoxification therapy. My dentist said it was okay.

It did not take long before I had problems with my lymph nodes and sinuses. These problems increased with every day, giving me a persistent clogged nose and severe neck ache. I got help from a curative practitioner who diagnosed an extreme mercury burden in my body. After years of diversions with various natural resources, I thought I was freed from my problem, and I felt better.

About half a year ago, I woke up with swollen eyelids every morning for over a week. I thought my lymphatic system was not right and started a daily lymph drainage to activate my lymphatic system. This was unsuccessful. I put on ice packs, which helped the swelling reduce somewhat, but I finally wanted a correct diagnosis for this health issue.

I sat down and was joined by my two helpful guides from the light side, Benny and Chico. "Hello, my dears, can you help me? I am at a loss and do not know what trigger is responsible for my swollen eyelids."

They immediately showed me a picture of my kidneys with the words, "Check your kidneys. They are still burdened with toxins and mercury that did not come out after detoxification. Activate them and drink lots of good water."

I thanked my beloved guides and went to my friend who was a very good and professional holistic medicine specialist. Through her special tests, she recognized the blockages in the body. I expected from her the same information as I had already received from my heavenly guides, Benny and Chico. My kidneys were not working well at the moment. They were contaminated with heavy toxins, including mercury. She gave me drops that activated my kidney function.

Shortly thereafter, my renal excretion activated, as indicated by a nightly walk to the toilet. The next morning, I woke up with perfectly normal eyelids. It is fascinating how exactly I received the message from my two leaders in the spiritual world. I thanked them, and they smiled at me.

CHAPTER 23

CAT BRUNO, THE HERO

Last summer, a lady contacted me. Her cat, Bruno, had been running away and disappeared for a few weeks. Could I help her? Unfortunately, another source of information confirmed for her that the cat had died, and that made her very sad. Nevertheless, she had gotten up the courage to ask me to communicate with Bruno.

I contacted the cat telepathically and found that he was alive—but very busy with himself and concentrated on getting food and shelter. Besides, he was tired. Therefore, I did not keep constant communication with him. The next day, the contact with him broke off altogether.

I sat down and asked my two guides, Chico and Benny, for help. They assured me that all was well, and I should trust my inner voice. There was no need to worry or fear. The cat was hungry, and he was hiding from dogs. I talked to the lady, reassured her, and motivated her to have confidence and to keep an eye out. The cat was alive.

I asked her not to be in the energy of fear. That would

be out of place. She could still make a prayer to Archangel Raphael. He was always there when you asked him and was especially a great help with lost animals. That calmed the lady very much.

I followed my inner voice, trusted the message from the spiritual world, and contacted Bruno the next day. The cat was weak and was near a farm. Shortly afterward, he was found by the lady's son. When Bruno made it home, he told me in detail about his great, brave adventures. It could not have been easy to steal a dog's food, and he had to hide in time.

He also emphasized that he would like to be outdoors. When he can sharpen his claws on a tree, creep in the tall grass, and observe the flying leaves and birds, he feels well. It is his grounding and his way of getting energy.

CHAPTER 24

GROUNDING

Animals are grounded in very different ways. Horses are happy with rolling on the paddocks. Dogs are happy with digging. Cats sharpen their claws with enthusiasm on a tree. Animals always strive to be in balance with nature and the earth, and this is fascinating and beautiful.

It is also important for us humans to be connected with the earth and be grounded. We are perfect in the present. If we feel physically or emotionally weak and want to run away from a problem, grounding is a very positive tool for getting back into the middle.

We can deal so much with spirituality—we are connected with the spiritual world—but we should not forget our physical being here in our body on earth. Stay on the ground, so to speak, and consciously feel completely connected with Mother Earth. Very often we are manipulated by external factors and directed to certain dramas and fantasies. With grounding, we can again switch off and free ourselves from the fog on the outside.

Grounding strengthens our immune system. We are fit, powerful, and emotionally balanced. We radiate satisfaction and harmony. Small problems we see as a positive force to get us back on the right path.

For me, hugging a tree allows me to absorb good energy. Through the terrestrial connection of the tree, I am automatically grounded. Any blocked energy gets released.

Walking barefoot is another good method of grounding, because the earth is directly connected with one's feet. As a child, I had enormous fun running barefoot, and I continue to do so. When I drive to the lake and walk barefoot, I profit from the additional purifying effect of the water. Many native human don't wear shoes and move barefoot through life. They live very connected with the earth.

Gardening is a pleasure for many people and also contributes positively to our need for grounding. It is a good idea to eat root vegetables and fruits that have grown in Mother Earth.

With my dog Chico, I was very often outside dancing. Chico loved it. He turned and danced around his own body very often. He laughed rightly, he was having so much fun. Of course, he motivated me to take part. The whole thing was supported with my singing and clapping. Both of us were completely free from blockades.

CHAPTER 25

SOCIAL NETWORKS

Fast text messages and social media conversations can cause many misunderstandings to arise. How, what, where? How was that meant? This instant form of communication can raise many questions.

I can sing several songs of it. How often have I been lost in the labyrinth of text messages? At the end, I did not know anything. There is, for me, only one thing to help: a clarifying personal conversation, or at least a phone call.

The conversations with my animals are clear. If I ask them, they provide me with detailed information. The images they send are honest, thorough, and without misunderstandings.

Should humans also enter the level of feeling, speaking, and perception, instead of using a small smartphone as a messenger? We were provided by the Creator with all the tools we need to communicate. We can feel with our hearts; we can speak, see, and hear. The only thing we need is to bring awareness to this level.

We have extremely fast technological advancements. Every year there are new, rapid developments in the computer field. Nevertheless, although many people are united, the personal contact is missing. Personal contact and the connection with nature seem less important than the time using the smartphone.

I am certainly not an adversary of technical progress. No, on the contrary, it is important for all of us and also very world-connecting. We should find a golden center and balance in order to be able to make use of both technology and our personal gifts.

CHAPTER 26

THE RIGHT TO BE LOVED

Through my many animal conversations, I completely turned into a balanced person who respects others and herself. I am in a new dimension of feeling and understanding. I live happily in the now and look forward to the future and what will come. In conflicts, I always recognize the positive aspects, which dissolve conflicts more quickly.

I try to help animals as a conversation partner, but I also try to help the owners through their animals and their conversations to solve old problems. I have noticed that many people are able to build up tremendous trust in me through the animal talks and have asked for help with their own conflicts. I thank and appreciate them for that. Very often, they were dealing with problems with parents, children, guilt, legacy, and past traces that were not yet processed.

As I love children very much, I asked Benny, "Do you have any special message about children?"

Benny gave me a message for children who are not recognized by their parents. It does not matter whether it is an adoptive child, a blood-related child, or children with physical or mental afflictions. Each child deserves the same love and attentiveness, and each child is equally loved, treated, accepted, and respected by the Creator.

Benny also gave me to understand that there is a father and mother in the essence of creation. It is our right to be loved as a child and adult, and it is also our right to treat ourselves as lovable people.

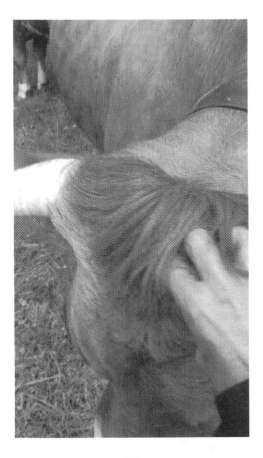

CHAPTER 27

CHRISTMAS IS IN THE AIR

Many know the annual turbulent events of the pre-Christmas period. As much as we turn and turn, it is and remains a challenge—still here and there a gift, some fast shopping, a few final preparations to get done. Everything should be perfect.

Thanks to my animal communication, I am more relaxed and in my own vibration at this time of year. A long queue in the supermarket, tense faces, even traffic jams can hardly influence my inner peace. I renounce perfectionism and smile.

Following the Christmas story, the Christ child was born in a modest accommodation in a stable, and it was still a wonderful event. I am sure that all those present, including the ox and donkey as well as the shepherds, were touched in their deepest heart.

It is said at Christmas that animals can talk about this night. With a smile, I can only say, "So then every day would be Christmas day for me." Somehow, that is not at all wrong. Every day we should praise and understand how precious it is to live in peace and harmony on this planet with all living creatures. We should not have to put up with Christmas but rest in the gentleness. This Christmas, I was able to share the joy of a small dog called Flip and its owners, and share with them as well.

It happened on December 24. Markus, Flip's owner, called me to say that Flip was refusing to eat. The dog was creeping, and Marcus could hear extreme bowel sounds. Recently, Flip had been treated for parasites in the intestines, which were no longer established according to veterinarians. Nevertheless, Markus was worried about Flip and thought there might be parasites again.

Flip, a very lively dog, was now constantly yawning and tired. Markus's wife was still at work, and he felt helpless. It was so close to Christmas, and he wanted a quiet and healthy Christmas.

Shortly thereafter, I started a conversation with Flip. The very sociable and talkative dog described to me its food as flabby meat. *It tastes terrible! Buh! Uhhh! Pooh!*

Flip was outraged, like a little boy who, instead of chocolate, got spinach on the plate. He wanted a great tasty Christmas dinner like a nice cooked piece of chicken. I told him that I would pass on his wishes. That Flip had parasites, I could not feel, nor was it transmitted to me by him.

When the owners got my information, they realized they had been giving him a new variety of fresh meat as a sample since yesterday. It was quite flabby and had no taste. So they knew the cause of Flip's unhappiness, and I could calm them down. I recommended a fine lean cooked piece of chicken with vegetables. Flip would be well and happy after that.

Later that day, I was sent a photograph by the owners. Flip had eaten a whole load of chicken. Now he was lying happily on the sofa, and it was a wonderful Christmas for all.

CHAPTER 28

COMMUNICATION IS THE KEY

I give my own advice from the animals. How wonderful it is that this was confirmed by the many thanks from my friends and customers. The animals always give me the power to control my thoughts, to be on the level of joy, to concentrate on the beautiful things, to pursue my path further, and to not be influenced by fearful media and energies.

With pleasure, I try to help animal owners and customers open their eyes and remove their old patterns. From my perspective and the animals', every single individual is important on this planet, and every little particle is significant. I compare it to the particles of a puzzle. Only a completed puzzle is perfect. Every particle, however small, has a task in this universe, and a place that is deserved and respected. Everyone is valuable.

Communicating with each other is an essential part. Communication is the key. Certainly, a quiet time of inner listening to our heart is also important. I practice and meditate every day. But in my opinion, if we do not communicate with each other, we cannot understand how others feel about and see a situation. We each have our own way of viewing things, and we can only come together through talking and compromising. Respect should be preserved.

I have never had a communication with animals where the animal has not preserved respect. They never offend, and so it is easier to communicate with them than with humans.

CHAPTER 29
CONCLUSION

The beginning is the end and the end is the beginning. And now, I am writing down the last lines for this book. I'm still thinking about my communication today with Chico. It touched me in the deepest part of my heart, and I hardly know how to write it in words—I am so moved by it.

Chico has decided to reincarnate. I will recognize him, and it will be done at the right time.

He sent me a picture of a young, life-threatened dog. A new window of time will open, and we will be allowed to experience a new path on this planet Earth—a path that transforms itself from the final touch into an even finer crystal path. The most important thing to know is that the path is flooded with love and light.

Notes

Notes

Notes

Notes

Notes

Notes

Notes

Printed in the United States
By Bookmasters